Time Goes By

A Day at an Airport

Sarah Harrison

Ⅲ Millbrook Press / Minneapolis

First American edition published in 2009 by Lerner Publishing Group, Inc.

Copyright © 2004 by Orpheus Books Ltd.

Millbrook Press
A division of Lerner Publishing Group, Inc.
241 First Avenue North
Minneapolis, MN 55401 USA

Website address: www.lernerbooks.com

Library of Congress Cataloging-in-Publication Data

Harrison, Sarah, 1981–
    A day at an airport / by Sarah Harrison.
      p.   cm. -- (Time goes by)
    Includes bibliographical references.
     ISBN 978–1–58013–551–1 (lib. bdg. : alk. paper)
    1. Airports—Juvenile literature. I. Title.
TL725.15.H37 2009
387.7'36—dc22   2007045534

Manufactured in the United States of America
1 2 3 4 5 6 — BP — 14 13 12 11 10 09

Table of Contents

 **THIS IS THE STORY** of a day at an airport. All the pictures have the same view. But each one shows a different time of day. Lots of things happen during this single day. Can you spot them all?

 **S**ome pictures have parts of the walls taken away. This helps you see inside the airport. Sometimes the side of the plane doesn't show. This is so you can see what's going on inside the plane.

As you read, look for people who appear throughout the day. For example, can you find the man who sleeps all day long? Keep an eye on one of the flight check-in people. He never seems to have any customers. Did you spot the stowaways? These people hide on a plane to get a free trip. Think about what stories these people might tell about being at the airport.

You can follow all the action at the airport from morning until night. The clock on each right-hand page tells you what time it is.

While the airport staff works, all sorts of other things are happening. Inside, travelers come and go. Some are asleep, waiting for their flights. Outside, a dog is on the loose. And luggage is being loaded. There's always something new to find!

Can you
find . . .

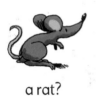

a rat?

Work starts early at the airport. It's still dark. But the cleaners are already busy. Some sleepy passengers have been waiting all night for their flight. Outside, a mechanic checks the plane's engine. He is making sure the plane is ready for takeoff. Security guards patrol the area. They find a stowaway hiding behind the aircraft. The rest of his friends escape the guards!

4:45 AM

Early morning

The day begins

A rock star arrives

Flight delay

Thunderstorm

Loading the plane

A president arrives

Nighttime

some suitcases?

a mechanic

Soon, the first passengers of the day board their flight.
Outside, workers load their suitcases. A stray dog has
wandered into the area. Two dogcatchers try to grab it.
Inside, a basketball team checks in for their flight.

6:00 AM

Early morning

The day begins

A rock star arrives

Flight delay

Thunderstorm

Loading the plane

A president arrives

Nighttime

Can you
find . . .

a waiter?

a cleaning woman?

It's still morning, but the airport is buzzing with excitement! A famous rock star is about to leave on her private jet. Photographers fall over one another trying to take her picture. Some young fans rush to ask for an autograph. Her bodyguards make sure that no one gets too close. Upstairs, a group of acrobats is waiting for their flight. Their circus tricks entertain the other waiting passengers.

Early morning

The day begins

A rock star arrives

Flight delay

Thunderstorm

Loading the plane

A president arrives

Nighttime

Can you
find . . .

a flight attendant?

the control tower?

a fire truck?

At lunchtime, a group of unlucky tourists finds out they are not going anywhere soon. Their plane's engine has a problem. They must wait for the mechanics to fix it. Two tourists lose their tempers. They start to fight. Other tourists stop them. A fuel tanker arrives to put gas in the plane. A fire truck waits nearby in case any gas fires happen. High above, in the control tower, are the air traffic controllers. They work hard to make sure all the planes land and take off on time.

12:30 PM

Early morning

The day begins

A rock star arrives

Flight delay

Thunderstorm

Loading the plane

A president arrives

Nighttime

Can you
find . . .

a check-in assistant?

a guitar player?

a luggage cart?

a dogcatcher?

huge thunderstorm takes place. No planes can take off in such bad weather. A few passengers decide to go upstairs for coffee while they wait. Unfortunately, a leak has started in the ceiling. Soon, water pours inside the airport. Outside, the airport workers quickly cover up the luggage. A couple of people don't seem to mind the rain. They stay outside and play in the puddles!

3:00 PM

Early morning

The day begins

A rock star arrives

Flight delay

Thunderstorm

Loading the plane

A president arrives

Nighttime

The rain has stopped. Planes can finally take off! An airline worker checks the passengers' tickets before they board the plane. They hurry through the tunnel and take their seats. A luggage truck brings their bags and suitcases to the plane. A sniffer dog finds a stowaway hiding with the baggage. Inside, a thief suddenly snatches someone's purse in the shop. He is caught!

5:00 PM

Early morning

The day begins

A rock star arrives

Flight delay

Thunderstorm

Loading the plane

A president arrives

Nighttime

Can you find . . .

a nun?

a sleeping man?

a reporter?

a skateboarder?

a photographer?

A visiting president has just arrived with his wife. Security guards watch carefully as they leave the plane. A car with dark windows is waiting to take them to their hotel. Photographers take pictures of the couple. A TV news team reports on their arrival. Inside, people try to catch a glimpse of the president. A group of nuns is waiting to check in. They sing to pass the time.

8:00 PM

Early morning

The day begins

A rock star arrives

Flight delay

Thunderstorm

Loading the plane

A president arrives

Nighttime

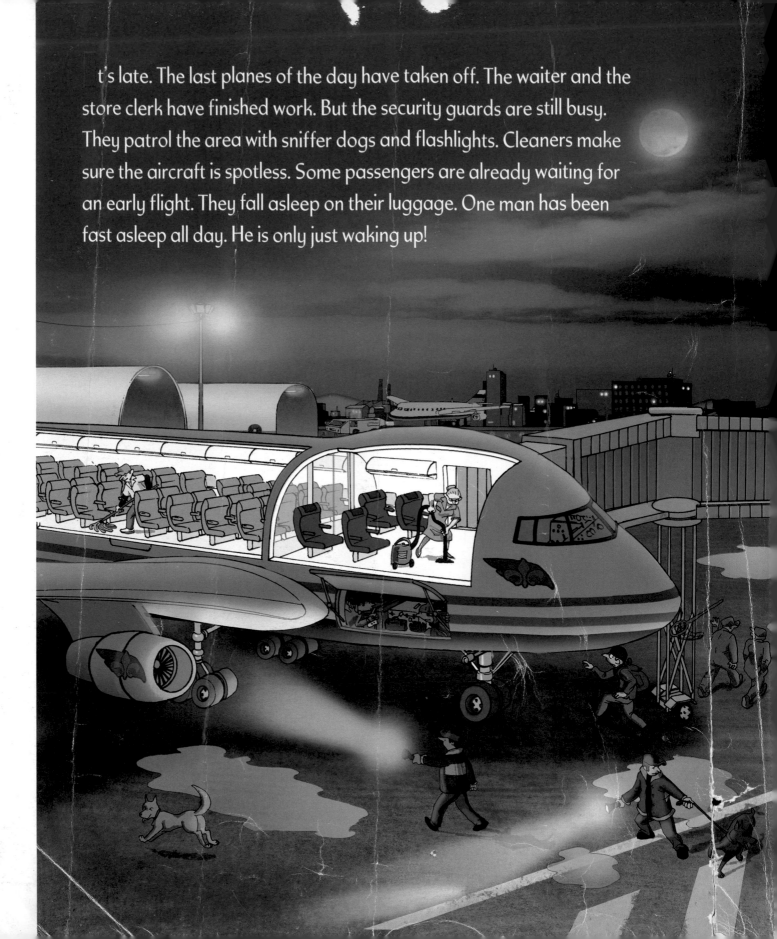

Can you find . . .

a stowaway?

the information desk?

a cleaner?

a waiting passenger?

some cats?

It's late. The last planes of the day have taken off. The waiter and the store clerk have finished work. But the security guards are still busy. They patrol the area with sniffer dogs and flashlights. Cleaners make sure the aircraft is spotless. Some passengers are already waiting for an early flight. They fall asleep on their luggage. One man has been fast asleep all day. He is only just waking up!

11:30 PM

Early morning

The day begins

A rock star arrives

Flight delay

Thunderstorm

Loading the plane

A president arrives

Nighttime

Glossary

air traffic controllers: people whose job is to keep planes landing and taking off safely. They are in touch with pilots by radio. The pilots are in planes on the ground and in the air.

bodyguard: a person who protects someone

clerk: a salesperson in a store

control tower: a tall building at an airport from which air traffic controllers talk to pilots

flight attendant: a person who takes care of passengers on a flight

fuel tanker: a truck that brings fuel to a plane

mechanic: a person who takes care of problems with engines or other machinery

security guard: a person whose job is to protect people and property from harm

sniffer dog: a dog that is trained to sniff for dangerous chemicals

stowaway: a person who hides on a plane to get a free trip

Learn More about Airports

Books

Hill, Lee Sullivan. *Jets.* Minneapolis: Lerner Publications Company, 2005.

Hill, Mary. *Signs at the Airport.* Danbury, CT: Children's Press, 2003.

Nelson, Robin. *From Metal to Airplane.* Minneapolis: Lerner Publications Company, 2004.

Santella, Andrew. *Air Force One.* Minneapolis: Millbrook Press, 2003.

Wadsworth, Ginger. *The Wright Brothers.* Minneapolis: Lerner Publications Company, 2004.

Waugh, John C. *The Kansai International Airport.* Danbury, CT: Children's Press, 2004.

Websites

Boeing Kids Page
http://www.boeing.com/companyoffices/aboutus/kids
Boeing is one of the world's largest builders of aircraft. The company's Kids Page has games, puzzles, and fun facts about how planes fly.

Classroom Resources at the National Air and Space Museum
http://www.nasm.si.edu/education/classroom.cfm
This site, part of the larger National Air and Space Museum, has quizzes, electronic field trips, and other activities for young pilots.

A Closer Look

This book has a lot to find. Did you see people who showed up again and again? Think about what these people did and saw during the day. If these people kept journals, what would they write? A journal is a book with blank pages where people write down their thoughts. Have you ever kept a journal? What did you write about?

Try making a journal for one of the characters in this book. You will need a pencil and a piece of paper. Choose your character. Give your character a name. Write the time at the top of the page. Underneath, write about what the character was doing at that time. Pretend you are the character. What are you doing? Are your activities hard or easy? Why? What have you noticed about the airport? Have you seen anything surprising? What?

Don't worry if you don't know how to spell every word. You can ask a parent or teacher for help if you need to. And be creative!

Index